BIGGER AND BETTER

Contents

Diana Bentley

Story illustrated by
Steve May

Heinemann

Before Reading

Find out about

- What eats what in the sea

Tricky words

- shrimp
- sea
- plankton
- catches
- sharp
- claws
- teeth

Introduce these tricky words and help the reader when they come across them later!

Text starter

In nature, little creatures are eaten by bigger creatures. In the sea the smallest living things are plankton. Plankton are eaten by shrimps. Shrimps are eaten by crabs. But what eats a crab?

What Eats What?

A shrimp lives in the sea.

A shrimp eats plankton in the sea.

Plankton are tiny plants and animals that drift in the sea.

But what eats a shrimp?

A crab eats a shrimp.

A crab catches a shrimp
with its sharp claws.

But what eats a crab?

A fish eats a crab.

A fish catches a crab with its sharp teeth.

But what eats a fish?

A shark eats a fish.

A shark catches a fish
with its very sharp teeth.

Quiz

Text Detective

- How does a crab catch a shrimp?
- What do you notice about each of the animals as you go through the text?

Word Detective

- **Phonic Focus:** Initial phonemes

  Page 3: Find a word beginning with the phoneme 'i'.
- Page 7: How many words are there in the sentence at the top of the page?
- Page 9: How do you know the sentence at the bottom of the page is a question?

Super Speller

Read these words:

as   be

Now try to spell them!

HA! HA! HA!

Q What day do fish hate?

A Fry-day.

11

In this story

 Lee

 Emma

Tricky words

- want
- spider
- eat
- bird
- tiger

Introduce these tricky words and help the reader when they come across them later!

Story starter

Lee and Emma are twins. They are great friends but one twin is always trying to be better than the other twin. One day, they were in the park. Lee saw an ant and said, "I want a pet ant."

I Want a Pet

"I want a pet ant," said Lee.

"I want a pet bird," said Lee.

"My bird will eat your spider."

"I want a pet cat," said Emma.

"My cat will eat your bird."

"I want a pet tiger," said Lee.

"My tiger will eat your cat."

"Your tiger will eat *us*!" said Emma.

"We don't want a pet!"
said Emma and Lee.

Quiz

- Why didn't Lee and Emma want a pet tiger?
- Why do the twins keep changing the pets they want?

Word Detective

- **Phonic Focus:** Initial phonemes
  Page 20: Find a word beginning with the phoneme 't'.
- Page 20: What words does Lee say to Emma?
- Page 20: Find a word that rhymes with 'beat'.

Super Speller

Read these words:

my   us

Now try to spell them!

HA! HA! HA!

Q Why do tigers eat raw meat?

A Because they never learned to cook.